THE MILLIONTH CIRCLE

JEAN SHINODA BOLEN, M.D.

THE
MILLIONTH CIRCLE

How to Change Ourselves and the World

THE ESSENTIAL GUIDE
to WOMEN'S CIRCLES

CONARI PRESS

First published in 1999 by Conari Press
Red Wheel/Weiser, LLC
York Beach, ME
With offices at
368 Congress Street
Boston, MA 02210
www.redwheelweiser.com

Cover illustration by Kathleen Edwards
Cover photo © PhotoDisc
Cover and book design by Claudia Smelser

LIBRARY OF CONGRESS CATALOGING-IN-PUBLICATION DATA

Bolen, Jean Shinoda.
    The millionth circle : how to change ourselves and the world :
  the essential guide to women's circles / Jean Shinoda Bolen.
        p.   cm.
    ISBN: 1–57324–176–8
    1. Women—Psychology.   2. Women—Social networks.   I. Title.
HQ1206.B55   1999
305.4—dc21   99–23769
                                                            CIP

Printed in the United States of America on recycled paper.

07 06 05 04 MV 10 9 8 7 6 5 4 3 2

THE MILLIONTH CIRCLE

1

ZEN AND THE ART
OF CIRCLE MAINTENANCE

. . . in the circles where we face ourselves,
we listen like a miracle,
and I reclaim the song which is mine. . . .

—Janice Mirikitani, *Where Bodies Are Buried*

ZEN AND THE ART
OF CIRCLE MAINTENANCE

THIS IS AN unusually short book for what it proposes, which is nothing short of changing the world and bringing humanity into a post-patriarchal era. It is written for women, who will be the ones to do it, if it is to be done. Though interested men are certainly welcome to read it.

The Millionth Circle was written to inspire women to form women's circles that have a center, and for women whose current participation in them will now be seen in this larger context. It is my contribution to accelerating a process and a movement that has already begun. It depends upon a simple hypothesis, whose mechanism has been proposed and observed, and is one that can be intuitively and immediately grasped: When a critical number of people change how they think and behave, the culture does also, and a new era begins.

Once the principles are understood, the significance of women's circles can be appreciated as a revolutionary-evolutionary movement that is hidden in plain sight. It appears to be just women getting together and talking, but each woman and each circle is contributing to something grander.

The Millionth Circle intruded itself on me while I was writing another book. I was working on the manuscript of *Goddesses in Older Women,* about the archetypes in women over fifty—one of which is not a goddess at all, but the archetype of the circle—when I wrote four pages of double-spaced thought, which was a complete and whole visionary statement. It felt as if its purpose was not to become several pages in a thick book, but rather that it go out into the world by itself, as an idea whose time has come. Within days, this perception was validated. Isabel Allende had asked me for ideas for a keynote lecture, and I faxed those four pages to her. When she quoted from them, the audience of 2,000 interrupted the talk with spontaneous applause.

Then came chapters 3 through 9, the "How to" portion of this book. For years now, as I encouraged women to form circles, I wished for an instruction book, a *Zen and the Art of Circle Maintenance,* which this is. These chapters have the visual appearance of poetry, and the number of words is quite sparse for such an ambitious undertaking.

The form came about when I serendipitously discovered the effect of using the centering feature instead of standard margins on my computer and, as a result, wrote a "How to" that drew images and words from the right side of my brain. I favored poetic rather than pedantic words, and then realized that the part of the reader's psyche that I wanted to engage speaks this language.

The perspective and insights in these chapters grew directly out of my own experience as a member of women's circles, going back to 1985. I've learned the most from two of these circles in particular. The circle that suffered a failure of trust and was abruptly dissolved taught me a great deal, maybe as much as the ongoing prayer/meditation circle that I've been in for fourteen years. The second source of experience about circles came from leading women's wisdom workshops. Every workshop I led was centered around meeting together in a large circle; each woman participant also was in a leaderless small group. A third contributing experience, for contrast, was as a member of boards and committees. From this, I could see how different and almost mutually exclusive each form is: one fosters the psyche, trust, and authenticity, the other facilitates productivity, the effective use of power, and persona.

During these years of being either a member or a leader of women's circles, I thought about circles and how they worked. The Jungian analyst-psychiatrist in me saw both psychological depth and growth, and how circles got in trouble and what kept them trustworthy. The part of me that appreciates how beauty and truth are linked saw how ritual and ceremony tapped into the imagination and were a medium for creativity and spirituality.

Those of you who have been in women's consciousness-raising groups or women's support groups may find that *The Millionth Circle* touches a place in your heart as you recall your group and remember the circumstances. I think you will also find that the "How to" chapters will be a reminder of what you know from that time. You have wisdom from this experience to bring to any new circle.

My focus is on the meaning of women's circles and their formation and maintenance because women as a gender have a natural talent for them. The circle is an archetypal form that feels familiar to the psyches of most women. It's personal and egalitarian. When the circle is taken into the workplace or community by women—often modified to be acceptable and unthreatening to men, who usually don't find this a natural form for them—it enhances collaborative undertakings and brings people who work together emotionally closer and in a less hierarchical relationship to one another.

Women whose previous experience with women's groups has left a bitter taste may need to revisit that old experience, with the perspectives here as a guide, before venturing into a new women's circle. The chapters on "A Circle Needs to Be Safe" and "A Circle in Trouble" may be especially helpful, and offer guiding principles for healthy circles, as well.

I hope that you will read chapters 3 through 9, which have the appearance of poems, as if they were, and that you will muse about what I have to say. Then your own insights and intuition will be evoked, amplifying their meaning. Poetry uses metaphors and analogies, draws from the symbolic level of the psyche, and is the language of the soul. Poetic imagery is also compressed information. Less can lead to more, if my words draw out what you and a circle of women together have as collective wisdom.

From what I have heard and observed, I believe that many women yearn to belong to a women's circle. If you are inspired to form a circle or deepen one, then this little book will be a boon to you, and to the circle that is formed or influenced by you. You will also be contributing to an evolutionary change in human culture—because your circle will be one more circle on the way toward "the millionth circle."

HOW TO CHANGE THE WORLD

2

The Millionth Circle

There is nothing as powerful as an idea whose time has come.

—Victor Hugo

Feminism catches fire *when it draws upon its inherent spirituality. When it does not, it is just one more form of politics, and politics never fed our deepest hungers.*

—Carol Lee Flinders,
At the Root of This Longing

HOW TO CHANGE THE WORLD

The Millionth Circle

"THE HUNDREDTH MONKEY" is a story that inspired antinuclear activists to keep on keeping on, when the commonsense view was that the nuclear arms race could not be stopped. The story and its moral was taken to heart as an allegorical tale based upon theoretical biologist Rupert Sheldrake's Morphic Field Theory: namely, that a change in the behavior of a species occurs when a critical mass— the exact number needed—is reached. When that happens, the behavior or habits of the entire species changes. The most widely read version of the tale was written by Ken Keyes, Jr., which I retell as follows:

> Off the shore of Japan, scientists had been studying monkey colonies on many separate islands for over thirty years. In order to keep track of the monkeys, they would lure them out of the trees by dropping

sweet potatoes on the beach. The monkeys came to enjoy this free lunch, and were in plain sight where they could be observed. One day, an eighteen-month-old female monkey named Imo started to wash her sweet potato in the sea before eating it. I imagine that it tasted better without the grit and sand or pesticides, or maybe it even was slightly salty and that was good. Imo showed her playmates and her mother how to do this, her friends showed their mothers, and gradually more and more monkeys began to wash their sweet potatoes instead of eating them grit and all. At first, only the female adults who imitated their children learned, but gradually others did also.

One day, the scientists observed all that all the monkeys on that particular island washed their sweet potatoes before eating them. Although this was significant, what was even more fascinating was that this change in monkey behavior did not take place only on this one island. Suddenly, the monkeys on all the other islands were now washing their sweet potatoes as well—despite the fact that monkey colonies on the different islands had no direct contact with each other.

"The hundredth monkey" was the hypothesized anonymous monkey that tipped the scales for the species: the one whose change in behavior meant that all monkeys would from then on wash their sweet potatoes before eating them.

As an allegory, The Hundredth Monkey holds the promise that when a critical number of people change their attitude or behavior, culture at large will change. What used to be unthinkable is done by some, and then many; once a critical number of people make that shift, it becomes what we do and how we are as human beings. Someone has to be a thirty-seventh monkey, and a sixty-third, and a ninety-ninth, before there is the hundredth monkey—and no one knows how close we are or how far away that hundredth monkey is until suddenly, we are there.

If you have ever walked a labyrinth, the journey is like this. You walk and walk, following a path that turns and changes directions over and over. You have no way of knowing how far it is to the center, until suddenly you are there. Once at the center—a symbolic place of insight and wisdom—you stay as long as you wish. Then it is time to take that knowledge or experience out into the world. And once again, you walk and walk the labyrinthine path, not knowing how close or far you are from the place you will emerge. Until you take that one last turn, and suddenly, you are out.

Like Imo and Her Friends

For human culture to change—for there to be a hundredth monkey—there has to be a human equivalent of Imo and her friends. For patriarchy to become balanced by the discerning wisdom and compassion that are associated with the feminine aspects of humanity, and by the indigenous wisdom and relatedness to all living things and to the planet, that shift will come in this hundredth-monkey way. I believe that this will happen when there are a critical number of women's circles: for patriarchy to change, there has to be *a millionth circle.* That's because what the world needs now is an infusion of the kind of wisdom women have and the form of the circle itself is an embodiment of that wisdom. Marshall McLuhan's famous expression, "The medium is the message," greatly applies to women's circles: a circle is nonhierarchical—this is what equality is like. This is how a culture behaves when it listens and learns from everyone in it.

In more ways than one, women talk in circles: conversation takes a spiral shape in its subjective exploration of every subject. Listening, witnessing, role modeling, reacting, deepening, mirroring, laughing, crying, grieving, drawing upon experience, and sharing the wisdom of experience, women in circles support each other and discover themselves, through talk. Circles of women supporting each other, healing circles, wisdom circles, soul sister circles, circles of wisewomen, of clan mothers, of grandmothers. Circles of crones, circles of pre-crones, lifetime circles and ad hoc circles, even circles of women in cyberspace and the business place, circles are forming everywhere. It's "Imo and her friends" getting together in circles, and learning how to be in one.

The more circles there are, the easier it is for new circles to form; this is how morphic fields work. Each circle is a regeneration of the archetypal shape and form that draws from every woman's circle that ever was, and each circle in turn adds to the field of archetypal energy that will make it easier for the next circle. Morphic fields and archetypes behave as if they have an invisible pre-existence outside of space and time, become instantly accessible to us when we align ourselves with that form, and are expressed in our thoughts, feelings, dreams, and actions. The circle is much more than the experience of this generation, a sacred circle especially.

See One, Do One, Teach One

See one, do one, teach one. When I was in medical school, this was the medical student mantra. This is how doctors learned procedures, an apprenticeship model of hands-on experience. Circle experiences are much the same, though it may be that the first circle you see is in your mind's eye and imagination. Then you might join a woman's circle or form one. Being in a circle is a learning and growing experience that draws upon the wisdom and experience, commitment, and courage of each one in it. Circles go through stages and changes, flourish or flounder, heal or hurt its members, and may be a transient experience or a lifetime one. Just as relationship skills carry over into circles, there is a vice versa; the circle experience can have a radically positive effect on relationships outside the circle, because it can provide a model—a place to practice honest and caring communication, until this is what you do and expect from others in your life. In this way, it can lead you to change the patriarchal structure of your relationships. As we begin to change our personal relationships, that change spreads. It's like throwing pebbles in a pond; each one has an impact and an effect, with concentric rings of change rippling out and affecting other relationships.

Changing Yourself and Your Share of the Patriarchy

If you suppress or put a lid on how you feel, minimize or deny what you see, or don't say what you want, and nobody in your life seems to notice, a circle is an egalitarian learning place. Just by being there. A circle that is trustworthy has a spiritual center and a respect for boundaries. It is a powerful transformer of the women in it. Circles also function as support groups; if you want to change something in your life or in yourself, it's a home base from which to go out and try. In a patriarchal climate, a circle of equals can be like an island of free speech and laughter. It makes us conscious of the contrast, through which we become aware of what we do to perpetuate the status quo, and how we might change it.

Every important relationship is a universe of two. Even though there are only two people in it, you are either in a circle or a hierarchy. If there is an unspoken assumption that you will defer or be subordinate and accept the other's judgment or choices in place of your own—you are living in a patriarchy of two. It is your particular share of the patriarchy, which can change if you do.

From One Circle
to the Millionth Circle

Being in one circle leads to being in others. In the same way that colonists in ancient Greece took coals from the fire in the center of the round hearth, from the home temple, with which to light the fire in the new temple, and a new bride took fire from her mother's hearth to light the fire in her new home, anyone who has been in a sacred circle can take that spirit—and that archetype and morphic field—into a new circle, or another part of her life.

You might move and form a new circle. Or not move, and start a second circle. You might speak of your circle to a friend, and be the inspiration for her to start a new women's circle. Or you may read this book, and decide that you want a circle to be in. The propagation of circles can, in this way, resemble the spread of strawberry plants: they throw out runners that put down roots and become new plants, until there is a field of them.

Women's circles form one at a time. Each circle expands the experience of being in one to more women. Each woman in every circle who is changed by it takes this experience into her world of relationships. Until, on one fine day, a new circle will form, and it will be *the millionth circle*—the one that tips the scales—and brings us into the post-patriarchal human era.

CASTING THE CIRCLE

Who, What, Where, When?

Until one is committed, there is hesitancy,
the chance to draw back, always ineffectiveness,
concerning all acts of initiative (and creation).
The moment one definitely commits oneself,
then Providence moves, too.
A whole stream of events issues from the decision.

Whatever you can do or dream you can,
Begin it.
Boldness has genius, power and magic in it.
Begin it now.

—W. H. Murray,
The Scottish Himalayan Expedition
usually attributed to Goethe

CASTING THE CIRCLE

Who, What, Where, and When?

To cast something has several meanings:

as in casting a net or a fishing line,

or as in casting a magic circle,

or as in casting a movie or a play

and selecting who will be in it.

How will this new circle take form?

O

A new women's circle begins with the idea or yearning

to be in a circle.

The image of a circle and the intent to form one

need to come together.

Is there heart, mind, and will for this creative work?

Tap into the inner stages of creativity:

Imagine, visualize, intuit, think of "who"

might be interested in being in a circle with a center.

○

If "who" might be in such a circle does not

immediately come to mind,

then "how" might potential members of a circle be found?

Like the first trimester of a pregnancy,

this is a tentative period.

Will forming a circle take hold as an intention?

Is there enough energy to carry it "to term"—into reality?

○

When there are two or more kindred spirits,

soul sisters, like-minded friends

to share the excitement and want a circle to happen,

there will be more creative energy to draw from.

○

In the planning and envisioning stage,

information helps.

Recall your own previous experiences with women's groups.

Think about what you have learned from them.

Read books about forming circles.

Talk to veterans of women's circles,

those who grew through them and those who survived them.

Ponder the idea.

○

Once pregnant with intention,

invite the creative spirit, grace, synchronicity, good fortune,

to bless this undertaking.

The Invitation:
Who Will Come?

Take the friends you have and bring them into a circle,

see if they have the interest and time

to continue to meet as a circle.

or

Trust your intuition and invite selected women

to a gathering to talk of forming a circle.

or

Run the idea of a circle by women you know,

invite those who are interested

to a gathering

to talk of forming a circle.

or

Start with two or three women,

each one invite one or two more

to a meeting to talk about forming a circle.

or

Begin with a discussion or work group you already have.

or

Gather at a retreat or a reunion or a conference.

Figure out logistics of time and place to meet later.

or

Have an "open casting call."

Invite any woman who is interested.

Announce the intention to form a circle

through a newsletter, bulletin board, the Internet, or however.

See who comes to the gathering.

○

Maybe the most expeditious way

of knowing who would want to form a circle with a center

is finding if *The Millionth Circle* struck a chord.

What Will the Circle Do?

Some have an agenda or a purpose,

an ostensible reason for meeting

beyond being a circle.

Quilting bees, for example.

Farm women met together and caught up

with each other's news.

I think many were mutual aid and learning societies,

were circles that happened to make quilts.

O

C. R. groups in the late '60s and '70s examined sexism,

identified patriarchy,

and found "the personal is political."

Some organized rallies and marches,

founded rape centers and battered women's shelters,

or published newsletters and magazines.

They were the heart of the women's movement,

mutual aid and learning societies,

that raised consciousness and empowered their members,

one woman at a time.

O

Today's version may call itself a discussion group,

or be a prayer or meditation circle, a study or support group,

or have a project or cause.

Whatever it is called,

whatever the agenda may be,

if it is a circle with a center

its members are witnesses, role models, and soul connections

for each other.

Providers of intangible spiritual and psychological support,

validators of reality and possibility.

Mutual aid and learning societies.

Agents of change.

The Place: Where to Meet?

Inside, outdoors, in a home or office,

a meditation room or studio,

in a living room or kitchen?

It is not where the circle meets but whether this can become

a sanctuary for the circle,

a place uninvaded by intrusive sounds, or by other people,

a "Do Not Disturb" location.

Where doors can be closed and silence is possible

and the raucous laughter and mirth of a women's circle

won't disturb anyone else, either.

Time: When Will the Circle Meet?

How often to meet, when, and how long?

The parameters of time determine who can be in the circle

and shape what can happen in the circle.

Some circles meet for two hours every other week,

Some every week,

Some circles meet on a weekend day once a month,

Some circles meet once a year at a reunion site,

and is "a same time next year" gathering.

Some now stay in touch with each other online,

and there are even "cybercircles" on the Net.

○

If there is a secret about how to make a circle,

it is that the women in the circle know

each other's personal stories,

know about each other's journeys,

know what is of consequence,

where the challenges and difficulties are

that matter.

For this,

time together over time is needed.

O

At the beginning of each new circle, however,

the questions are

How often? When? And how long?

Something about the amount of time

divided by the number of women,

while not a mathematical formula with any guarantees,

is a realistic consideration.

4

CENTERING THE CIRCLE

In the sweet territory of silence we touch the mystery.
It's the place of reflection and contemplation, and it's the place
where we can connect with the deep knowing,
to the deep wisdom way.

—From a talk by Angeles Arrien,
author of *The Four-Fold Way*

CENTERING THE CIRCLE

When a women's circle is centered,

it is in the shape of an invisible wheel or mandala.

The circle meets as if around a sacred fire

at the center of a round hearth.

The center is what makes a circle special, or sacred.

The invisible center

as source of energy, compassion, and wisdom.

How to kindle this fire and keep it glowing?

○

Begin the circle

with something that centers it.

Value quiet

as the means of centering.

○

The connection to the center is intuitively felt,

purely subjective.

In silence or singing or hum,

each woman connects with her own center,

connects with the center of the circle,

and feels like both a spoke and a part of the rim.

Invisibly part of a wheel,

connected to everyone else in the circle through the center.

This is what makes the circle a sacred place.

This is what makes the women in it,

even if initially strangers, feel at home.

○

Once women have gathered together in a circle,

there may be a period of gestation.

A time of forming and growing

as each woman decides for herself whether or not

she will make a commitment of her time and her Self

to the circle.

○

Centering the Circle:
Preparation

1. Create an altar space around which the women will meet.

2. Going from social chatter to sacred circle

begins with getting everyone's attention:

With a sound? Words?

Think ahead about how this will be done.

3. Once there is attentive quiet,

centering requires another shift,

from outer to inner focus.

Think ahead about how to introduce this and when.

4. Remember that the comfort level of everyone matters.

Anything new or unfamiliar needs to feel safe and not weird.

5. Remember that the first circle meeting is the beginning.

Whatever is done at the first meeting

influences subsequent ones.

When creating something new, the beginning matters.

6. You are creating a circle with a center.

Keep an image of spokes of a wheel in your mind

or the archetype of a fire at the center of a round hearth,

because an archetype energizes the circle.

○

Centering the Circle:
What You Can Do

Centering can be facilitated by the sound of a bell,

or a drum, or by humming or singing,

or by a few minutes of silent meditation, or by words.

Or by lighting a candle, or visualizing a center.

Holding hands around a center literally creates a circle,

an act that can also be spiritually centering.

Re-center the circle by any of these means, when need be.

For circles and people get off-center at times.

A CIRCLE OF EQUALS

Groups run by and for women are our psychic turf;
our place to discover who we are, or who we could become,
as whole independent human beings.

Somewhere in our lives, each of us needs a free place,
A little psychic territory. Do you have yours?

—Gloria Steinem,
Outrageous Acts and Everyday Rebellions

A CIRCLE OF EQUALS

The circle is a principle as well as a shape.

It goes counter to the social order, pecking order,

superior/inferior, ranking order

that compares each individual woman to others.

Sitting in a circle, each woman has a physical position

that is equal

to every other woman in the circle.

She takes her turn and the circle turns,

she speaks up and is heard.

Still old habits prevail, until the practice of equality

makes equality the expected norm.

Creating a Circle of Equals
Is a Work in Process

The idea of a circle of equals is held as a common intention.

Each woman is committed to developing and maintaining it,

for herself and for the circle.

Every woman in the circle matters to herself and to the circle.

Every woman contributes to the circle by her presence,

and when she speaks, by what she discerns and shares.

○

Once the circle is formed,

any significant decision needs to be made

by a process of consensus.

This only works if there is honesty.

If one fears to be truthful, lest feelings be hurt

or punishment follows,

there is codependency.

Codependency and equality are incompatible.

○

Silence is consent.

If one woman dominates the circle

and takes up "all the air in the room,"

it is not she alone, but she and everyone else

who are equally responsible.

Each woman speaks only for herself

and not as if for the others in the circle.

Each woman has a responsibility to the circle

to pay attention to what is going on in herself and in the circle,

and to speak up.

○

In any circle, some are more verbal, faster to react, and quicker

to arrive at a conclusion than others.

Balance comes from hearing from everyone.

Practicing Equality

Check In and Go Around.

Each in turn speaks to the questions,

How are you, really?

What concerns you most now?

Depending on the situation, on the woman, and on the circle,

it may be health, relationships, work, creativity,

spiritual life, or politics.

In this way, over time, we are witnesses to each other's lives.

We know what is truly important

and the nature of each one's personal journey.

We feel the pain, celebrate with joy, and are kin.

Sometimes we have ideas and suggestions,

as an equal to an equal,

which is not doing therapy nor infantilizing.

O

The Talking Stick.

This is borrowed from our indigenous relations.

In their councils, the elders and clan mothers meet in a circle

to discuss a problem or decide what needs to be done.

In their councils, listening is as important as speaking,

thus silences matter, and one speaks only after deliberating.

Like Quakers.

O

I imagine they are having inner conversations,

or listening for inner guidance,

every bit as much as they are listening to each other.

When an elder decides she is ready to say something,

she picks up the talking stick and speaks.

As long as she holds the talking stick, she has the floor,

and is not interrupted.

O

Sometimes, the talking stick is used in a circle of equals,

when there are problems to face within the circle,

because it helps slow the deliberations,

and allows silences in between.

With a talking stick, we listen more intently

and usually shape our thoughts, before we speak.

With a talking stick,

we are calling upon the wisdom, honesty, and compassion

that exists in the center of the circle, and in us.

○

The "talking stick" may not be a stick at all,

anything consecrated or intended for this,

a symbolic object for example, serves the purpose.

○

Ask for Input from a Silent Member.

If something is going on and she hasn't spoken up,

does she have an insight or feelings about it?

Is what has been unsaid the missing piece?

Maybe she is attuned to the center.

Maybe she is aware of the shadow.

Might what she has to say be what the circle needs to hear?

Or might silence be what is called for,

and saying nothing be her contribution.

We won't know unless we ask.

○

Maybe she is a like a silenced Cassandra,

unpracticed at having her perceptions heard,

or unused to saying the truth with tact and kindness,

or having an equal voice.

In a circle with a center, this is something for all to learn

through practice.

○

M U S I N G S

Sometimes I think of improvisational music

especially that quintessential American form called *Jazz*

as the music most like a women's circle

that is "cooking," flowing, making music together.

Each woman a separate instrument,

playing separately together,

sometimes wailing, sometimes reaching highs,

sometimes melodic, always in the moment.

Each is making variations on a theme

or taking tangential flights of self-expression

that become part of the range or depth of the composition.

There becomes an awareness of the whole,

and of being an equal,

contributing to the music.

○

To pay attention in a circle as in improvising music

is to know when to come in and solo,

and when to provide backup with a listening heart.

Playing together as equals takes practice and presence.

6

A CIRCLE NEEDS TO BE SAFE

In safe relationships,
you can trust that you will not be lied to
and will be free of exploitation,
where the other does not feel superior at
your expense,
does not betray your confidences,
or intrude upon your boundaries.

—Jean Shinoda Bolen, *Ring of Power*

A CIRCLE NEEDS TO BE SAFE

A circle is a shape with an unbroken circumference

and a symbol of wholeness.

The boundary edge or line defines the circle.

Once it is broken, it's no longer a circle.

The same principle holds for a women's circle.

The boundary must be intact for it to be a circle,

and for it to be safe.

That boundary is the ability to hold the contents,

a necessity for trust to exist.

What is said in confidence is held in confidence.

Plain and simple.

○

It is otherwise a meeting of women

who do not trust each other,

a gathering of women in whose company

one wears a persona and social armor.

This is not a sacred circle.

○

For a women's circle to be safe,

what is said must be treated with respect,

however painful or shameful a confession,

however juicy it would be as gossip.

Self-revelation takes courage and trust,

which must be honored

and held in confidence.

Lest you fail her, yourself, and the circle.

What is not shared and remains a shameful secret

keeps you/her beyond the pale.

Outside of the circle of acceptance.

Unhealed.

○

For a women's circle to be safe it must be a womb space

for new possibilities

where the woman and her dream can be supported

when it is barely formed and still in the dark.

When the psyche of a woman is pregnant

with an idea of what she could do

or become.

Ridicule aborts what could have come forth,

indifference starves it.

A safe circle holds the dream of what she could be

in confidence

and nourishes the possibility.

M U S I N G S

A circle with a center is not therapy

even if healing happens within it.

What is not shared in the circle that hurts the circle

and makes the woman who withholds it feel unsafe

belongs there.

Not everything else does.

7

A CIRCLE IN TROUBLE

Show up or choose to be present.
Pay attention to what has heart and meaning.
Tell the truth without blame or judgement.
Be open to outcome, not attached to outcome.

—Angeles Arrien,
The Four-Fold Way

A CIRCLE IN TROUBLE

Women's circles get into the same kinds of difficulties

that women have in other relationships,

especially friendships.

○

Trust may be shaken or betrayed

after something said in confidence was not held in confidence.

There may be personality clashes, negative projections,

anger, judgments, and hurt feelings.

○

Sometimes a lack of commitment is the problem

that is subtle and eroding.

If a member of the circle is habitually absent or late or leaves early

or treats the circle as an option,

when it is a high priority for the rest,

the effect on the circle is like a small hemorrhage over time,

or a small leak in a boat.

Energy leaks out.

Resentment and withholding seep in.

○

A circle may be filled with palpable tension,

or may become a superficial ladies' group,

mouthing insincerities.

Sometimes a wonderful circle for a number of years

becomes stagnant,

as if reaching a "this far and no further" place.

○

A member's alcohol, abusive relationship,

emotional, or physical problems

may overwhelm the circle

if its members forget that it is not a therapy group

and can't fix these problems.

But even so, a circle can be a major caring influence

when the situation is honestly and compassionately faced,

and the truth is spoken that help is needed.

And support for getting help is what the circle can do.

○

One woman's problem

is a variation of another's past history,

or a reminder of an another's painful childhood,

or is similar to something going on in another's current life.

To acknowledge this may be an opportunity

to see the effect that such (once forbidden) conversations

can have,

when truth is called forth.

○

The only other alternative, as in life,

is for the circle to become dysfunctional.

Then its members fail to address the situation in the circle,

and the subject becomes the unmentioned

"elephant in the living room"

and judgmental talk goes on outside the circle.

○

Attendance may become "iffy,"

when avoidance is what is being practiced

rather than truth.

Maybe it's a relief when a particular person does not show up,

Or something feels wrong,

even if nothing shows on the surface.

Then the circle is acting like a dysfunctional family,

whose members are afraid to speak up

about how uncomfortable or powerless they feel.

Each in her own way gets into a practice

of not being totally present.

Denial is not a river in Egypt.

○

Sometimes a woman does not belong in this circle

because she can't make the commitment to really be there.

As in any significant relationship

ambivalence and the inability to make a commitment

become problems.

○

Sometimes a woman does not belong in this circle

because she cannot hold onto her center

or connect to the center of the circle,

or keep confidences,

or see others or herself clearly,

and she needs to leave for the good of the circle.

The same problem arises for women in their

codependent relationships.

○

Abandonment and autonomy issues arise

when a woman is ready to leave the circle

for her own good reasons

and the others feel abandoned, guilty, or angry.

How can she leave without doing damage

to herself and the circle,

without undoing the good feelings?

○

There is a time to face what is true and take action.

To do what is right for yourself against opposition.

To not stay (in any relationship) for the wrong reasons.

Maybe this is the lesson for yourself and for the circle.

Whether unilaterally or as a circle,

it is hard to initiate leave-takings and endings

that may not be mutually desired.

○

Sometimes facing what needs to be said and needs to be done

becomes an unexpected turning point,

not an end.

○

Sometimes a circle that appears to be in trouble

is really at the end of a life cycle,

has served its purpose and its members

and is winding down.

This is a crucial time before completion

when the truth of the situation

needs to be discerned.

Trouble comes

if the thought of dissolving the circle

is judged as subversive

and is not voiced.

○

Acknowledging what is so

makes completion possible.

Allows us to reflect upon

what we experienced, witnessed and learned

in the circle

and express gratitude.

Such endings are a time to mourn what is passing,

celebrate completion,

and graduate together.

How to Keep a Circle Healthy

In principle,
each member attends to her own psyche and to the circle.

O

1. Each keeps the intention and image of the circle with a center

in mind,

especially when there are difficulties.

O

2. Each seeks her center, in meditation and silence,

prays for wisdom, compassion, discernment, and courage

for herself, and for the circle.

O

3. Each examines the state of her own psyche

whenever she feels off-center,

or the circle does,

and considers possibilities that she is part of the problem:

Am I projecting my shadow onto someone?

Is this a familiar polarized state I get into—is it my complex?

○

4. When the energy in the circle feels "off,"

anyone can ask for silence

for each woman to check-in with herself:

How am I?

and inquire into the state of the circle:

How does it feel? What is going on?

When it's a minor misalignment,

the check-in time usually reconnects the circle to the center.

If there is a major problem still to be resolved,

this is the time for each person to speak up

about how the circle feels and how she is

and what the circle might do next.

○

5. If what was said in the circle was not held in confidence,

it is a boundary problem for the circle

(and not only a problem between two of its members).

If it is not brought up and resolved

the circle is not safe for anyone.

○

6. If one person dominates the circle,

it is a problem for everyone.

Remember that this is a circle of equals.

Each needs to go to the center for wisdom and discernment,

for compassion and courage.

Each needs to speak up and name the problem

that it is, for herself.

When there is a problem in the circle

if one woman speaks her truth

there is a strong possibility that she speaks for others

who are silent

or speaks for a silenced part in others.

○

7. Once we see how our actions appear and affect others,

the problem we may be to others may be solved.

A circle of women is a multifaceted mirror

in which each sees herself reflected.

What she sees of herself in the words and faces around her

depends upon the capacity of each woman as mirror

to be clear and compassionate.

What we see depends upon the quality of the mirrors

and the lighting,

which can be kind to us or not, however true the image.

What we see in ourselves, we can work on changing.

○

8. When the problem is letting a woman go

when she is ready to leave the circle,

the solution begins with acknowledging feelings,

however irrational.

Suppose there is anger or guilt,

or feelings of abandonment or depression—

(that really belong to an unhealed loss from the past)

Then this insight is a parting gift.

A leave-taking needs to be worked through,

and have a ritual to mark its significance

for the women and for the circle.

○

9. When a woman has a problem that is too much

for the circle,

the separation from the circle is harder.

Not just for the women who leaves under such circumstances,

but on the circle as well.

Both need to "bite the bullet" as the excision is done,

and work on healing after.

Maybe something will help, maybe nothing will

but time.

○

10. Remember that a women's circle is not perfect.

M U S I N G S

In the circle, as in life,

the most valuable lessons often come

through having done the best we could do

with the most difficult circumstances.

The circle and its members grow in depth

through its hardest times.

"That which doesn't kill us, makes us strong."

○

The archetype of a circle may be perfect.

A women's circle never is.

But if it holds its center when troubles arise

and there is wisdom, love, and honesty

and room for making mistakes,

the circle is more than "good enough."

It is a creative work of art

in process.

CEREMONIAL CIRCLE

I am a circle
I am healing you.
You are a circle
You are healing me.
Unite us
Be as one. . .

—Women's spirituality song,
         composer unknown

CEREMONIAL CIRCLE

A women's circle draws upon our sense of beauty and form

expressed through the rituals that open and close the circle.

Just as there is a beginning and an end to every poem,

which a circle can be said to resemble.

A free-form poem, certainly,

but boundaried by the opening and closing,

by the time reserved for this special gathering,

that becomes comfortingly familiar.

○

The circle has an invisible center,

a sacred fire at the center of a

round hearth.

Ancient Greeks called this source of light and warmth Hestia,

the divine feminine at the center,

Goddess of the Hearth and Temple.

○

A women's circle has a visible center, which is an altar space.

It may be empty or have a Zen simplicity

or hold symbolic objects of personal meaning.

Like the table prepared for a seder meal,

the altar space is recreated each time.

For this is a ceremonial circle, a sacred ritual,

a gathering of women involved in an art form

that can change us and our world.

○

A circle is women inventing their own rituals and celebrations,

their own rites of passage,

celebrating birthdays and traditional holidays,

or the seasons and the solstices,

whatever it is that has meaning.

○

Rituals, altars, celebrations—whenever there is ceremony

there also must be vigilance

against obligatory, empty form.

It is not what is done, but the spirit in which it is done

that makes all the difference.

○

(Including the possibility that nothing will show

that this is a circle and not a meeting,

and all is held in the psyches of those in the circle.

No bells or whistles, drums or candles.

Nothing but women together.

The essence of a women's circle is invisible anyway.)

The Ceremonial Touch

A Candle or Candles at the Center

One new votive candle

or one special candle, lit anew each time.

Or as many candles as there are members of the circle.

A special candle holder, candles floating in a bowl.

Or even a lighted wick of an oil lamp.

Each is a visible symbol of an invisible fire,

that is spirit, soul, wisdom, illumination, heart.

the fire around which we gather.

○

An Altar Cloth

Something colorful or beautiful,

that may have been created for just this use,

or perhaps a scarf

transformed into an altar cloth for this occasion.

On which there might be a candle, or flowers, or anything.

○

Calling the Circle

The shift from conversation to circle,

the shift from mundane into sacred space,

needs more than the announcement that "it's time to meet."

A ceremonial touch

can bring this about.

Some circles begin by holding hands and becoming still.

Some by a sound: a Tibetan bell, a singing bowl,

or a drum beat.

Some borrow from an indigenous ritual

and use the smoke from sage,

some by music or with a chant.

Some have words that are ritually said

to open the circle and invite the spirits in.

Or align to the four directions and to Earth and Sky.

Like everything else about women's circles,

There is no one way to do it.

○

Ceremonies and Celebrations

"Ask for what you need,"

may be a significant personal ritual.

a rite of passage or transition.

Rites of passage are about the cycles of life,

to mark endings and beginnings.

It could be

a croning ceremony to claim the archetype of the wisewoman,

a celebration of something new of yourself into the world.

It could be

the beginning of a medical descent into the underworld

of surgery, chemotherapy, the unknown.

Tell your story, what this means,

this time of transition or potential transformation.

It could be

a ritual to mark the end of a relationship,

or bring an end to a time of mourning.

Ask for the blessing of the circle,

as you go beyond the boundaries

of your known world,

move into a new phase, reinvent yourself.

A ritual is a creative act, performance art,

as elaborate as high church,

or as simple as a silent observation.

○

Ending the Circle

Just as there are ways to open the circle,

so are there ways to close it.

Words, ritual, sound, quiet,

Blow out the candle,

Keep faith in each other

Until we meet again.

M U S I N G S

Pilgrims in the Himalayas

who encounter each other on a mountain path,

clasp their hands together in that universal gesture of prayer,

bow, and say, *"Namaste."*

"The divinity in me greets the divinity in thee."

("The goddess in me beholds the goddess in thee.")

Namaste.

Rituals are just elaborations of this.

THE MILLIONTH CIRCLE

Never doubt that a small group of thoughtful, committed citizens can change the world; indeed, it is the only thing that ever has.

—Margaret Mead

THE MILLIONTH CIRCLE

Western civilization is the story of patriarchy,

a dominator, hierarchical history of power and intellect

that together have brought us to new heights of technology,

and to the possibility of destroying our planet.

○

Our rain forests are being slashed and burned.

Our air, water, and land polluted.

Nuclear waste, ground-poisoning chemicals,

hydrocarbons, and toxic aerosols

poison our Mother the Earth,

ourselves, and all creatures large and small.

Toxicity and indifference

damage chromosomes, make holes in the ozone,

result in air so thick that many gasp and cough

as they breathe.

○

Profit and power as the ruling principles,

lead to this

and to wars.

Are creating a wasteland.

The Grail Legend Is a Planetary Story

The Grail Legend tells us of the Fisher King

(symbol of power and patriarchy).

He has a wound that will not heal,

and a kingdom that is a wasteland.

When he is healed the land will be, too,

but only the grail can heal him.

○

Most think it is a chalice,

the goblet used by Jesus at the Last Supper,

when he said the words of communion,

"This is my blood—do this in remembrance of me."

Which has not healed the wasteland.

○

In the rite of the Mass, only a priest could hold this cup

(because "only men were made in the image of god").

Never a woman.

And yet in the Grail Legend,

It's always the woman, the Grail Maiden,

who holds this chalice,

symbol of the sacred feminine,

a womb filled with blood

that disappeared from the world.

○

In myths and dreams and in our collective memory,

women are remembered as they once were and could be:

carriers of the sacred feminine.

If the patriarchy is to be healed and the planet restored,

might women's wisdom be needed?

○

The Premise and the Power of the Millionth Circle

Start with women's circles,

each one is like a pebble thrown in a pond.

The effect on women in them,

and the effect women in them have,

send out concentric rings of influence.

See one, do one, teach one.

Be an influence where you are.

If enough women learn from each other,

and change their behavior,

like Imo and her friends,

in the story of The Hundredth Monkey,

the way things are done and what is believed

can change.

O

Remember history?

Remember how one age ends and another begins?

The Age of Faith, The Age of Reason,

The Reformation, The Renaissance,

even The Age of Anxiety.

Historians break time into Ages and Epochs,

Acknowledging that major shifts take place.

What "was and always will be" in one age,

Is outmoded, superceded, revised

in the next.

O

A peaceful revolution is going on,

a women's spirituality movement, hidden in plain sight.

Through circles of women, healing women,

Might the culture come around?

○

There is no "always was, always will be"

in human affairs.

Something like a teeter-totter effect happens

at certain points in time.

Rupert Sheldrake's Morphic Field Theory is enacted

and history changes.

When a critical mass—the hundredth monkey,

or the millionth circle—tips the scales,

a new era will be ushered in

and patriarchy will be over.

You have noticed that everything an Indian does is in a circle, and that is because the Power of the World always works in circles, and everything tries to be round. . . . The sky is round, and I have heard that the earth is round like a ball, and so are all the stars. The wind, in its greatest power, whirls. Birds make their nests in circles, for theirs is the same religion as ours. . . . Even the seasons form a great circle in their changing, and always come back again to where they were. The life of man is a circle from childhood to childhood, and so it is in everything where power moves.

—Black Elk,
Oglala Sioux Holy Man

About the Author

Jean Shinoda Bolen, M.D., is a Jungian analyst in private practice, Clinical Professor of Psychiatry at the University of California Medical Center, San Francisco, an internationally renowned lecturer, and author of the bestselling *Goddesses in Everywoman, The Tao of Psychology, Gods in Everyman, Close to the Bone, Crossing to Avalon,* and *Ring of Power.*

Dr. Bolen is an advocate for women, women's issues, and ethics in psychiatry, a Fellow of the American Psychiatric Association, past chairperson of the APA Council of National Affairs, and a former board member of the Ms. Foundation for Women. She is in two acclaimed documentaries, the Academy Award-winning antinuclear film *Women—For America, For the World* and *Goddess Remembered.* She lives in Mill Valley, California.

Join the Millionth Circle Campaign!

Become a member of the Millionth Circle community and help change the world.

Register your circle as part of the growing community of women's circles:

www.millionthcircle.com

For more information on Jean Shinoda Bolen, M.D., visit her web site:

www.jeanbolen.com

CONARI PRESS, established in 1987, publishes books on topics ranging from psychology, spirituality, and women's history to sexuality, parenting, and personal growth. Our main goal is to publish quality books that will make a difference in people's lives—both how we feel about ourselves and how we relate to one another.

Our readers are our most important resource, and we value your input, suggestions, and ideas. We'd love to hear from you— after all, we are publishing books for you!

To request our latest book catalog or to be added to our mailing list, please contact:

CONARI PRESS
368 Congress Street
Boston, Massachusetts 02210
800-423-7087   fax: 800-337-3309
e-mail: orders@redwheelweiser.com
www.redwheelweiser.com